Contents

This page intentionally left blank.

Section One
Roadmap Overview

Statistical test and analysis methodologies provide many benefits to the DoD Test and Evaluation (T&E) community. These benefits include:

- Design of Experiments (DOE) that elicit the maximum information from constrained resources.

- Avenues for maximizing information learned from testing and integrating information across multiple tests.

- Defensible rationales for test adequacy and quantification of risk as a function of test size.

Despite these benefits, statistical test and analysis methods have not been universally or consistently applied within the DoD T&E community. The 1998 National Research Study "Statistics in Defense, Acquisition and Testing" concluded that, "major advances can be realized by applying selected industrial principles and practices in restructuring the paradigm for operational testing…" and that "…the current practice of statistics in defense testing design and evaluation does not take full advantage of the benefits available from the use of state-of-the-art statistical methodology." Dr. J. Michael Gilmore, Director, Operational Test and Evaluation, agreed that there was much to be gained by applying state-of-the-art statistical tools to test and evaluation and has pushed to increase the rigor of operational test and evaluation.

The Test Science Roadmap effort chronicled in this report officially began in January 2011 with the development of the Roadmap Committee Charter. The overarching goal of the Test Science Roadmap was to increase the scientific and statistical rigor of test and evaluation. This document summarizes the accomplishments of the past two years. The Roadmap Committee Charter identified six specific goals, which are summarized below.

Goal 1: Assess the current state of analytic capabilities within each of the Service Operational Test Agencies (OTAs).

- All roadmaps need a starting point. Assessing the analytical capabilities within each of the OTAs provided a baseline for this roadmap. This report summarizes the structure and manpower of each of the OTAs. The report recommends that all of the OTAs will benefit by increasing their numbers of civilian employees having advanced degrees in scientific, technology, engineering, and mathematics (STEM) fields.

Goal 2: Develop qualification guidelines for personnel performing test design and analytic services for different kinds of T&E organizations.

- The education and training section of this report highlights an appropriate educational program. All OTAs should have access to at least one subject matter expert with an advanced degree in statistics, operations research, or systems engineering.

1

Goal 3: Develop a roadmap for training, education, and other support that Services and Agencies will need to attain the required test design and analytic capabilities.

- Each of the OTAs and DOT&E have implemented training programs. These training programs should continue to be updated with best practices and lessons learned.

Goal 4: Develop case studies of the implementation of scientific test design across the test program.

- This report includes over 20 full case studies and examples spanning all warfare areas. Additional case studies are described and available.

Goal 5: Provide guidance for the documentation of test design and statistical rigor in Test and Evaluation Master Plans (TEMPs), Test Plans, and Reports.

- DOT&E developed a TEMP Guidebook that provides guidance on the documentation of statistical rigor in TEMPs and Test Plans. A recommendation for the future is to capture the best methods for preparing test reports using statistical methods.

Goal 6: Form a permanent DOT&E Advisory Board to advise on best practices for incorporating statistical rigor into test planning and analysis of test results.

- Over the past year, the Roadmap Committee has served as an advisory board for DOT&E. This group should be codified into a permanent advisory board that meets regularly to ensure best practices and lessons learned are disseminated both to DOT&E and across the Services.

The Test Science Roadmap Committee membership was composed of DOT&E, Deputy Assistant Secretary of Defense (Developmental Testing and Evaluation (DASD(DT&E)), the Service OTAs, the Service T&E Executives, and advisors from the academic community. The effort was multi-faceted. Figure 1-1 shows the key elements of the Test Science Roadmap, which strongly emphasized statistical methods and tools for planning and analyzing tests. The emphasis on statistics, particularly DOE methods, reflects (1) the general applicability of statistics across the T&E of all systems, (2) the potential for large returns on investment made possible by employing statistical methods in T&E, and (3) the need for a rigorous approach to assessing test adequacy and determining how much testing is enough. In addition to emphasizing statistical methods, the roadmap sought to encourage engineering understanding of the systems under test, since the scientific principles that govern system performance are imperative to planning rigorous tests.

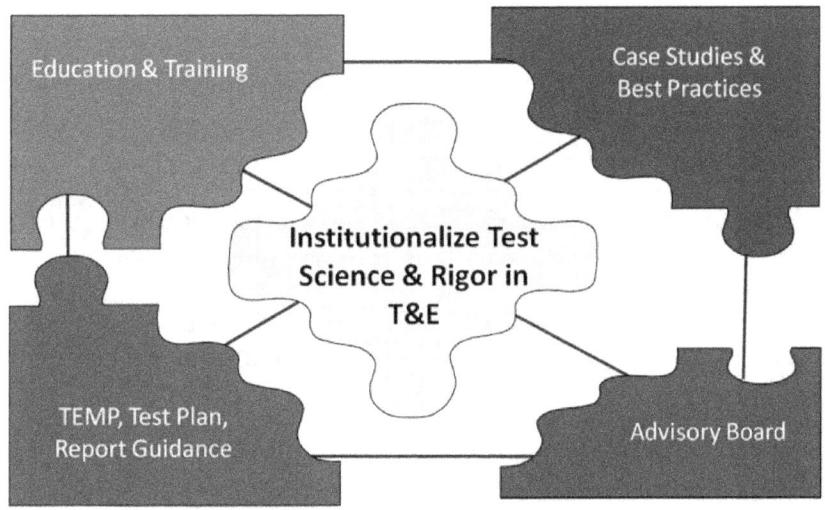

Figure 1-1. Roadmap Focus Areas

This report documents the progress we have made in the past two years, summarizes the current state of DoD analytic capabilities and the major steps forward in the past several years, and makes recommendations for the future. While the roadmap was officially designated as a two-year effort, the effort to institutionalize test science in the DoD began before this roadmap and will continue for many years to come.

Figure 1-2 captures some important milestones on the road to institutionalizing scientific rigor in T&E. These milestones are discussed in more detail below.

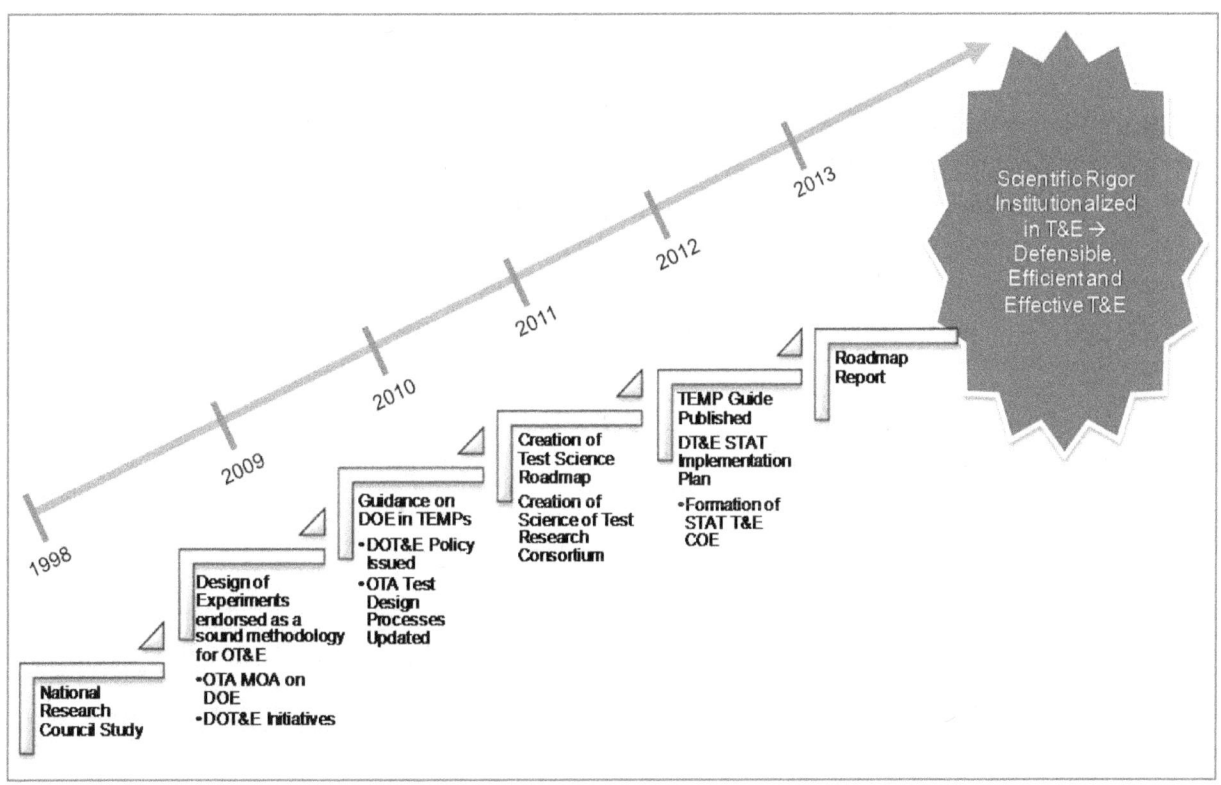

Figure 1-2. Major Events in the Test Science

3

National Research Council Study

In 1998, the National Research Council noted the inadequate use of statistics in T&E. The study "Statistics, Testing, and Defense Acquisition: New Approaches and Methodological Improvements" contained several key recommendations and conclusions:

- Major advances can be realized by applying selected industrial principles and practices in restructuring the paradigm for operational testing.

- The current practice of statistics in defense testing design and evaluation does not take full advantage of the benefits available from the use of state-of-the-art statistical methodology.

- All estimates of the performance of a system from operational test should be accompanied by statements of uncertainty through use of confidence intervals.

- The Service test agencies should examine the applicability of state-of-the-art experimental design techniques and principles and, as appropriate, make greater use of them in the design of operational tests.

- OTAs should promote greater attention to the specification of statistical models for equipment reliability, availability, and maintainability, and support for the underlying assumptions.

These recommendations provided an initial path for the DoD T&E community to integrate statistical rigor into the DoD acquisition processes.

Operational Test Initiatives

In 2009, the OTAs (in collaboration with DOT&E) took the next major step on the path to incorporating statistical rigor into T&E when they signed a memorandum of agreement with DOT&E endorsing the use of DOE "as a discipline to improve the planning, execution, analysis, and reporting of integrated testing." Additionally, in 2009 Dr. Gilmore, DOT&E, highlighted DOE in his initiatives. He noted that DOE was applicable across both developmental and operational testing and that DOE allows us to quantify "the confidence level of the test, the power of the test, and some measure of how well the test spans the operational envelope of the system."

However, despite the endorsement of DOE by the OTAs and DOT&E, there still were disagreements and inconsistencies in how to apply DOE in operational testing. In 2010, Dr. Gilmore issued guidance on what to include in TEMPs and Test Plans, outlining his expectations for those documents and for the definition of a rigorous test planning process.

DOT&E TEMP Guidebook

In February 2011, DOT&E published a TEMP guidebook highlighting the substantive content DOT&E is looking for in TEMPs; the guidebook was an extension to and embedded in the Defense Acquisition Guidebook with which all DoD acquisition personnel are familiar. The

TEMP Guidebook is available on the DOT&E public website (www.dote.osd.mil). Specifically, it provides guidance on many test science topics, including:

- Design of Experiments
- Mission-oriented metrics
- Reliability growth
- Modeling and Simulation
- Information Assurance

The TEMP Guidebook is just one of the many guidance and policy documents that have incorporated test science topics. This document and others are described in more detail in the Policy and Guidance section of this report.

Scientific Test and Analysis Techniques

DASD(DT&E) is also working to incorporate more scientific and statistical rigor into developmental T&E. In a parallel and closely-related effort in January 2012, DASD(DT&E) signed a seven-year, three-phase implementation plan for institutionalizing scientific test and analysis techniques (STAT) in test and evaluation. The implementation plan was signed by the Service T&E Executives and DOT&E. The STAT Implementation Plan expands upon DOT&E's initiative to increase the rigor of T&E into the DT&E community and seeks to support the needs of the DT&E community, addressing the wide variety of tests conducted within DT&E. The two organizations are following the same key elements shown in Figure 1-1. In particular, DASD(DT&E) has stated that the use of STAT will generate T&E efficiencies; provide rigorous, defensible T&E strategies and results; and improve the level of knowledge for developmental test planning, execution, and the analysis process.

One key component of the STAT Implementation Plan is the establishment of a STAT T&E Center of Excellence (COE). The STAT T&E COE provides program managers with statistical, scientific, and test expertise for 20 initially selected programs across all of the Services. This document discusses the accomplishments of both the Test Science Roadmap and the STAT implementation team for improving test science in education/training, case study and best practice development, policy and guidance, and the formation of advisory groups.

Report Overview

In the past two years, we have made significant progress towards institutionalizing test science in T&E, but there is still a long way to go before we are taking full advantage of all of the state-of-the-art scientific methodologies that the scientific community has available for T&E. This document summarizes the gains that have been achieved in the past two years and provides recommendations for the future.

The second section of the report summarizes the state of the OTA workforce and makes recommendations for how each OTA can enhance its workforce to support the initiative of increasing scientific rigor in T&E. This is followed by a section on major policy and guidance changes made by DOT&E to incorporate more rigor in the planning, conduct, and analysis of T&E. The report also includes a summary of both the training and education courses available to the T&E workforce, and descriptions of the recent Institute for Defense Analysis (IDA)-developed, DOT&E-provided training materials for OTAs and DOT&E action officers.

Of particular interest is the case studies section of this report. It includes a short summary of many recent acquisition programs using scientifically rigorous T&E. Each case study illustrates one or more best practices and/or lessons learned that DOT&E has developed over the past two years when applying advanced statistical and scientific method to T&E. The appendix to this report provides each case study in more detail.

The section on Requirements in T&E summarizes DOT&E's work engaging the requirements community over the past year. The report also discusses a vision for a future advisory board leveraging two existing groups, the STAT COE and the Science of Test Research Consortium. The report concludes with suggested recommendations for the future as DOT&E continues to champion further improvements to the scientific rigor of T&E.

Section Two
Assessment of Current Workforce Capabilities

The first step in implementing the Test Science Roadmap was to assess the current state of analytical capabilities within the Service Operational Test Agencies (OTAs). The data that appear in this chapter reflect the OTA workforce population as of September 30, 2012. The OTAs are:

- The Air Force Operational Test and Evaluation Center (AFOTEC),

- The Army Test and Evaluation Command (OT Elements) (ATEC),

- The Commander, Operational Test and Evaluation Force (COTF),

- The Marine Corps Operational Test and Evaluation Activity (MCOTEA),

- The Joint Interoperability Test Command (JITC), and

- The Special Operations Command (SOCOM) J8-O.

DOT&E has monitored the demographics of the OTA workforce using the Defense Manpower Data Center (DMDC) military and civilian personnel records since 1990. The educational backgrounds of the personnel of each OTA are of particular importance because implementing test science requires personnel with scientific backgrounds and the ability to understand the systems under test.

For this roadmap report, we extracted the occupational and educational profiles of current military and civilian employees in the OTAs and concluded that in order to continue progress in institutionalizing rigorous test and analysis techniques, all of the OTAs could benefit by increasing their numbers of civilian employees with scientific, technology, engineering, and mathematics (STEM) backgrounds in their workforce. Additionally, each OTA should have access to at least one subject matter expert with an advanced degree in statistics, operations research, or systems engineering. For the military workforce, the OTAs should continue to recruit officers with operational, fleet experience vice acquisition professionals.

Figure 2-1 shows that the total manpower in the OTAs has been relatively constant over the past 10 years, albeit the civilian workforce has declined since FY08 after increasing from FY02 – FY06. Note that contractor personnel data are not included in workforce demographics.

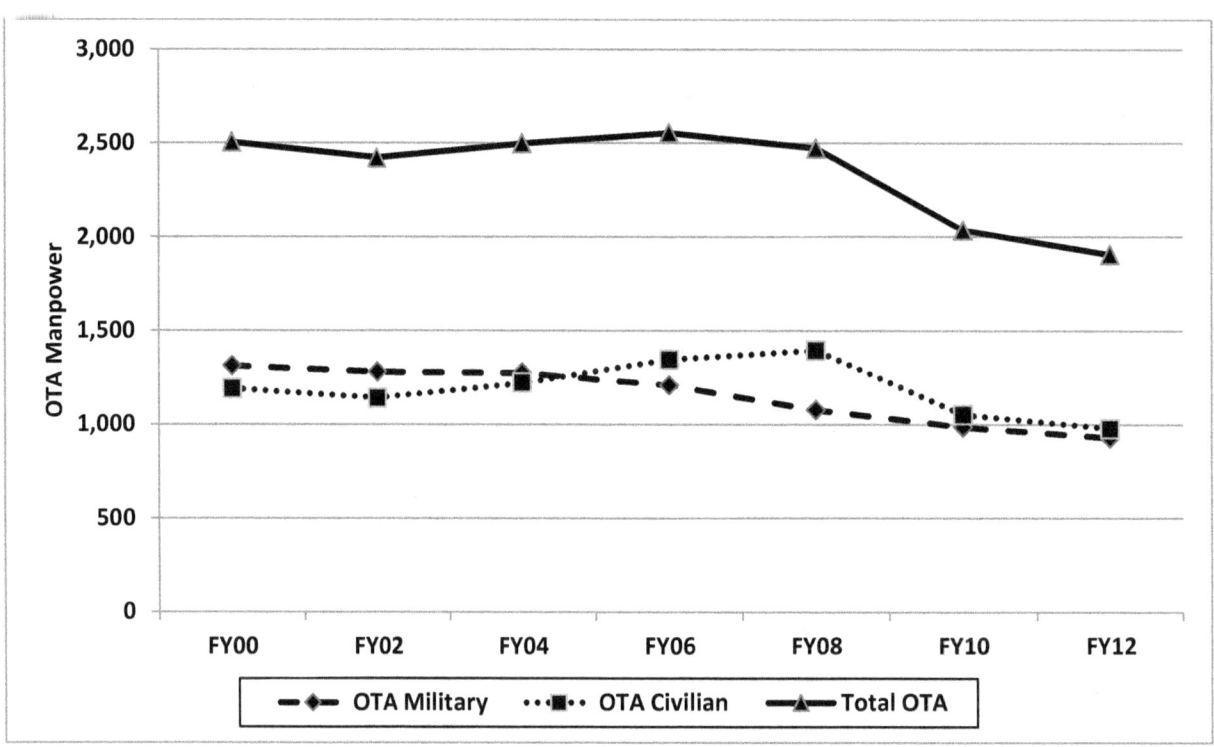

Figure 2-1. OTA Manpower 2000-2012

Figure 2-2 provides a perspective of how the OTA civilian workforce fits into the overall DoD test and evaluation (T&E) workforce. Figure 2-2 depicts the civilian totals for the OTA workforce, the Under Secretary of Defense (Acquisition, Technology, and Logistics) (AT&L) workforce in T&E coded billets, and the Major Range Test and Facility Base workforce. Of note in Figure 2-2 is the area denoted with a double asterisk, indicating that there are approximately 600 OTA civilian personnel in acquisition-coded billets. The top 10 units with acquisition workforce coded personnel totals 589 civilians out of a total of 977 civilians, or 60 percent. This is up considerably from a few years ago when the total acquisition coded civilian personnel was less than 50 percent. Over 300 of the personnel are at the Army Evaluation Command with another 160 between Army Operational Test Command, JITC, and Army Test and Evaluation Command. The Air Force has 75 personnel (out of the top 10 units) and the Navy has 14. A similar analysis of the military workforce shows the top 10 units with acquisition coded military personnel have a total of 339 out of 928, or 36 percent of the military personnel in the OTAs are acquisition professionals. The top unit is COTF with 109 officers or nearly all of COTF's 117 non-administrative military workforce.

In general, the expertise at an operational test command should come from officers and, to some extent civilians, having an "operational" career field vice an "acquisition" career field. Such experience supports two facets of operational test. First, operationally-qualified personnel lend their expertise to the evaluation of operational effectiveness and suitability. While many quantitative metrics are examined during an operational test, the summation of those metrics to an effectiveness and suitability evaluation is primarily assessed by "operators" current in that area of combat. Second, in order for the evaluation to remain "independent" or free from conflict of interest, the evaluator should not be concerned that their next assignment may have them working within the command structure of the organization sponsoring the system being evaluated.

Additionally we note that in order for civilian personnel to qualify for training within the Defense Acquisition community, they must be coded in one of the defined acquisition workforce "career fields" – one of which is the "T&E career field." Personnel with this designation are required to maintain their technical currency within the field through a formal certification process. It is DOT&E's position that the OTA workforce should remain impartial to the acquisition programs that they examine and that T&E workforce education/training should be focused on technical disciplines supportive of the T&E mission.

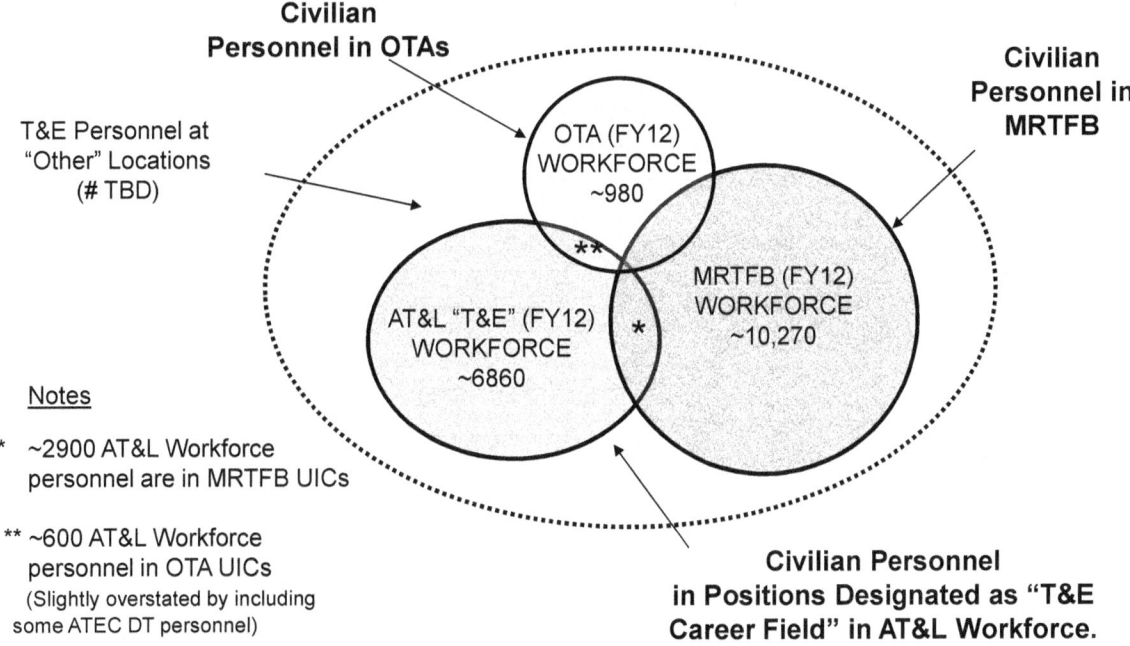

Figure 2-2. T&E Workforce Venn Diagram (FY2012)
(Overlap not to scale)

Table 2-1 summarizes the OTA civilian manpower by Service as of September 30, 2012. Although the DMDC personnel data are comprehensive, personnel data alone cannot be used to compare the OTA organizations.

The size of the Service OTAs varies from MCOTEA with 84 personnel, to ATEC with 934 personnel. COTF, with a complement of 297 personnel, and AFOTEC, with 590 personnel, fall in between the two extremes. The size of an OTA is a function of several factors, including the number of OT&E programs managed, the size of those programs, and the complexity of those programs. The business plan and organizational structure established by each Service also influence the size of each OTA. Note also that JITC and SOCOM personnel resources supporting OT are nominal and are excluded from the demographic analyses.

Table 2-1. OTA Manpower by Service, 2012

Service	OTA	Units	Military Strength	Civilian Strength	Total Workforce	Contractor Work Years
Army	ATEC	13	307	627	934[a]	412
Navy	COTF	7	224	73	297[b]	140
USMC	MCOTEA	2	28	56	84	59
Air Force	AFOTEC	17	369	221	590	42
TOTAL			928	977	1,905	653
			48.7%	51.3%		

[a] Totals represent those military and civilian personnel associated with the operational test mission, not the entire ATEC organization.
[b] Numbers do not include personnel in the VX squadrons

Figure 2-3 reflects the military and civilian census over a span 10 years.

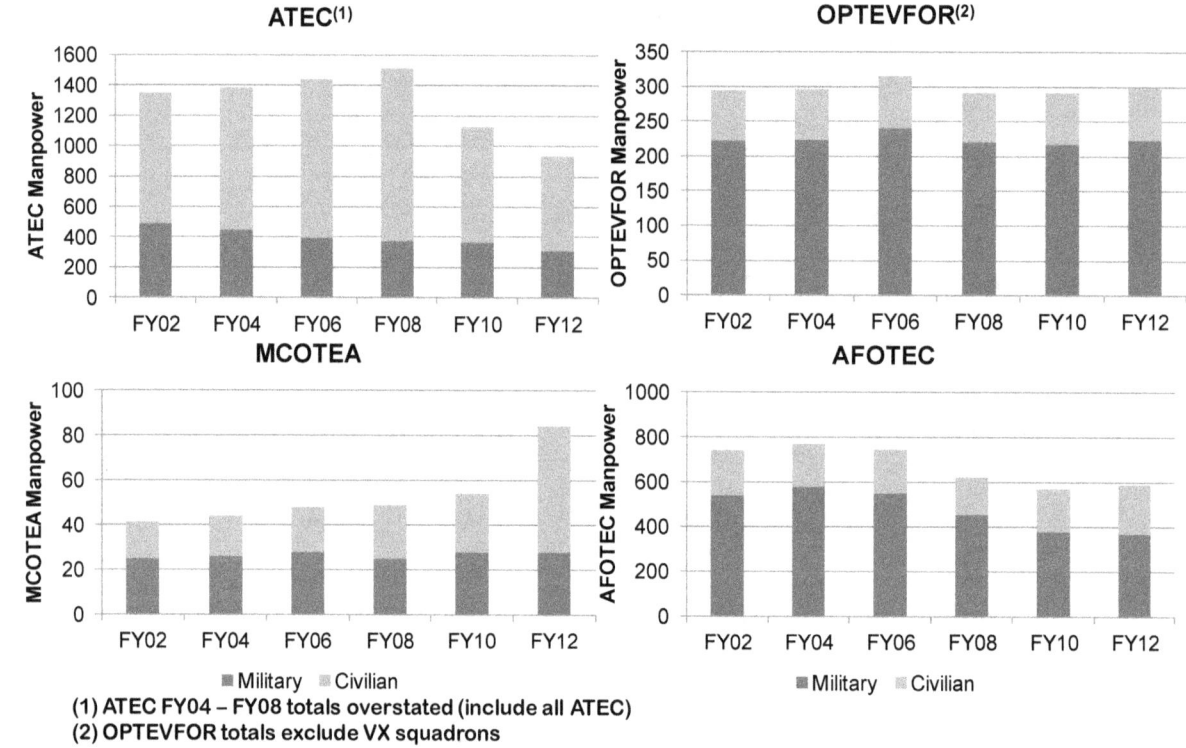

(1) ATEC FY04 – FY08 totals overstated (include all ATEC)
(2) OPTEVFOR totals exclude VX squadrons

Figure 2-3. Service OTA Workforce Census FY00 – F12 Trends

ATEC has the largest organization because of the scope of their activities. ATEC, in addition to managing and conducting OT&E, manages and conducts developmental test and evaluation (DT&E), owns test ranges, and includes a separate organization of independent evaluators; however, he numbers in Table 2-1 and the rest of this section only include those personnel that are associated with operational testing, although some of the evaluators in the Army Evaluation Command may support some DT&E as well as OT&E. ATEC currently (FY13) manages 94 DOT&E oversight programs in addition to JUONS and DT&E programs.

MCOTEA, the smallest OTA, has fewer programs than other OTAs because the Army and Navy manage and conduct OT&E for many of the Marine Corps' large vehicle, weapon, and aircraft programs. MCOTEA currently (FY13) manages 77 DOT&E oversight programs.

COTF manages all Navy OT&E, which encompasses 244 programs.

AFOTEC currently manages 75 DOT&E oversight programs. Unlike other OTAs, AFOTEC predominantly manages Acquisition Category (ACAT) I, ACAT II, and DOT&E oversight programs. AFOTEC occasionally conducts OT for ACAT III programs when requested by a Major Command or other users such as security forces, but smaller programs are generally conducted by Air Force Major Commands.

Table 2-2. Number of Personnel and Programs on DOT&E Oversight List per OTA

Service	OTA	Total Personnel	ACAT1	ACAT2	Other	Total	Average # Personnel per Oversight List Program
Army[a]	ATEC-OT	934	45	8	41	94	**9.9**
Navy[b]	COTF	297	79	35	130	244	**1.2**
USMC[c]	MCOTEA	84	17	2	58	77	**1.1**
Air Force[d]	AFOTEC	590	32	6	37	75	**7.9**

[a] Personnel associated with OT provided by ATEC; evaluators that work DT and OT may be included
[b] Additional personnel from VX squadrons not included
[c] Additional personnel from air detachments not included
[d] Additional personnel from major commands not included

The number of personnel in each of the OTAs does not fully reflect the number of personnel involved in OT&E programs. COTF often uses "trusted agents" not assigned to COTF that are not included in their workforce totals. For example, although the Navy VX Squadrons and a Marine Air Detachment are not under COTF administrative control, they are operationally controlled by COTF. Those units account for over 600 personnel not reflected in the COTF totals cited above. Likewise, Air Force Major Commands provide support for AFOTEC OT&E events; flying hours are funded under Air Force training, not OT&E. For ATEC, the Brigade combat team supporting the twice-yearly Network Integration Evaluations is not included in the ATEC organization.

Although comparison is made complicated by the different structures of the OTAs and the level of detail in the DMDC data, Table 2-2 shows the total personnel and number of programs each OTA manages, as discussed above. The average number of personnel per program is likely biased low for the Navy, Marine Corps, and Air Force due to their reliance on other operational squadrons for test assets and test conduct.

While there are differences in the number of personnel assigned to the different OTAs, each Service has different policies and organizational practices that drive those differences. All the OTAs follow the same policies set forth by DOT&E, but the implementation of those policies are Service-unique. For example, funding of OT&E programs is different for each OTA. For ATEC, the Material Developer budgets for test funding of all DT and OT ACAT I programs; the Program Manager/Program Executive Officer budgets for ACAT I (IC and ID) and ACAT IA (IAM and IAC) systems. ATEC budgets for OT of ACAT II, IIA, III, and IV systems. Operational Maintenance Activity budgets for all Follow-On Operational Test and Evaluation. For COTF, the developing agency budgets for all resources identified in the approved Test and Evaluation Master Plan. AFOTEC has separate Program Elements for most OT&E (AFOTEC only conducts OT&E of ACAT I and DOT&E oversight programs). There are case-by-case exceptions for large OT&E programs over $8M.

Educational Background of OTA Personnel

The educational background for each OTA is of particular importance because implementing test science requires personnel with technical backgrounds and the ability to understand the systems under test. Tables 2-4 and 2-5 provide the distribution of educational degrees by Service in 2012 for civilian and military personnel, respectively, omitting personnel in the Administrative Occupational Category.[1] Figure 2-4 shows the distribution of college degrees for the combined military and civilian personnel at each OTA. ATEC and AFOTEC have the highest ratio of advanced degrees in their OTA workforce. We note that there are no civilians with Ph.D.s at COTF. DOT&E is aware that COTF has supplemented this need by using contractors.

Table 2-4. OTA Officer-level Civilians
Non-Administrative Occupational Categories Only
Educational Profile

DMDC Occupational Category	AFOTEC				ATEC				COTF				MCOTEA			
	ND [a]	B.A./B.S.	M.S.	Ph.D.	ND	B.A./B.S.	M.S.	Ph.D.	ND	B.A./B.S.	M.S.	Ph.D.	ND	B.A./B.S.	M.S.	Ph.D.
Engineering and Maintenance	3	10	19	0	14	132	81	3	3	1	11	0	0	2	2	0
Science and Professional	2	5	23	5	3	116	124	10	1	6	3	0	0	2	5	1
All other non-Admin Civilians	5	3	13	1	18	16	12	2	0	1	1	0	8	12	9	0
Total	10	18	55	6	35	264	217	15	4	8	15	0	8	16	16	1
Percentage of OTA non-admin Workforce	11%	20%	62%	7%	7%	50%	41%	3%	14%	30%	56%	0%	20%	39%	39%	2%

[a] ND: No degree; indicates the number of personnel holding less than a 4-year college degree.

---

[1] One of nine officer/officer-level occupational categories in the DoD occupational taxonomy, specified in DoDI 1312.1-I.

Table 2-5. OTA Military Educational Profile
Non-Administrative Occupational Categories Only

DMDC Occupational Category	AFOTEC				ATEC				COTF				MCOTEA			
	ND [a]	B.A./ B.S.	M.S.	Ph.D.	ND	B.A./ B.S.	M.S.	Ph.D.	ND	B.A./ B.S.	M.S.	Ph.D.	ND	B.A./ B.S.	M.S.	Ph.D.
Engineering and Maintenance	1	35	44	0	11	21	22	0	2	1	3	0	0	0	0	0
Science and Professional	2	18	31	5	0	18	8	0	0	1	0	0	0	0	0	0
All Other Officers	0	18	89	2	1	53	52	0	16	48	46	0	1	10	10	0
Total	3	71	164	7	12	92	82	0	18	50	49	0	1	10	10	0
Percentage of OTA non-admin Workforce	1%	29%	67%	3%	6%	48%	55%	0%	15 %	50%	82%	0%	5%	48%	48%	0%

[a] ND: No degree; indicates the number of personnel holding less than a 4-year college degree.

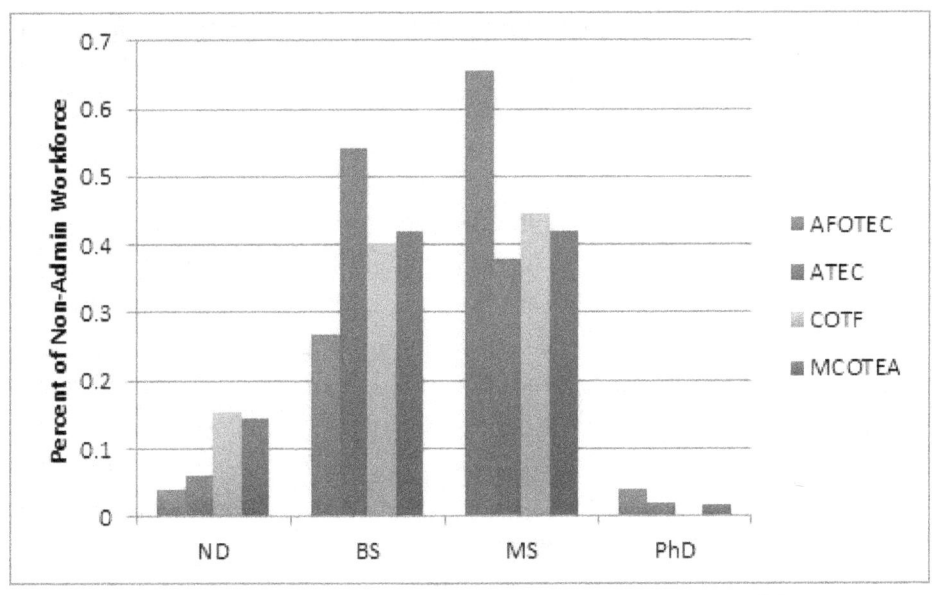

Figure 2-4. Distribution of College Degrees per OTA

Not only is the level of education important to assessing an OTA's capability to support test science, the type of degree is important as well. Degrees in STEM provide a strong understanding of the scientific method and the analytical skills important to rigorous T&E. Additionally, degrees in statistics, operations research, and systems engineering are especially useful when constructing designed experiments and analyzing data from tests.

Table 2-6 displays the numbers of these targeted degree fields that focus on the test design and analysis.

**Table 2-6. Number of Civilian Personnel with Degrees in Fields
Suited to Test Design and Analysis**

Degree Area	AFOTEC	ATEC	COTF	MCOTEA
Mathematics/Statistics	5	53	0	4
Computer & Info Science	13	71	8	1
Engineering	37	242	9	0
Engineering Technology	7	23	1	0
Biological Sciences	1	13	1	0
Physical Sciences	6	20	3	1
Total (Percent of Non-Admin Personnel)	69/89 (76 %)	422/531 (79 %)	22/27 (81 %)	6/41 (15%)

Of note is the lack of civilian personnel with degrees in the Mathematics/Statistics Instructional programs in the Navy.

Other Observations

Each OTA includes both military and civilian personnel. The two components are essential and the split between military and civilian employees has been relatively even over the past 10 years. Active duty personnel with operational experience bring military expertise and understanding of current operations and Service needs, whereas the civilian personnel bring specific civilian skill sets that include expertise in engineering and science. Civilians also infuse the testing profession with long-term corporate knowledge and specific analytical capabilities that are not typically a focus of military career tracks. Ideally, the two components complement each other at an OTA; however, DOT&E has observed that the civilian workforce comprises personnel with many of the same skills and experience as the military personnel. This might be the result of a tendency to hire back Service members as civilian employees after they retire from the Service. Regardless, the result of this trend is that OTAs have a tendency to be overpowered by Service expertise and underpowered in STEM-field-specific analytical capability.

Recommendations

All of the OTAs could benefit from increasing their numbers of advanced degrees in STEM fields. This is especially true for COTF, which should consider hiring several civilian Ph.D.-level advisors in targeted degree areas.

Indeed, each OTA should strive to have a higher percentage of STEM degrees in the civilian workforce. This is in line with the new AT&L/DT&E requirement for T&E certification requiring acquisition workforce T&E career field personnel to have a specific STEM degree to receive T&E certification.

Section Three
Policy and Guidance

Prior to 2010, there was no guidance or requirement to use statistics-based techniques in the conduct of test and evaluation. Policy that supports the use of scientific test techniques is essential to ensuring a continued commitment to test science. This section documents the recent policy and guidance updates that support the use of statistically based test and evaluation.

Both DASD(DT&E) and DOT&E have supported the inclusion of more detailed language in 5000.02 in terms of test science. The DT&E enclosure of the current draft version of 5000.02 requires that:

> *"The TEMP should describe the scientific and rigorous approach to designing an efficient test program that will characterize system behavior across a variety of conditions."*

And the OT&E section requires:

> *"Every TEMP will include a list of independent variables (or conditions, parameters, factors, etc.) that may have a significant effect on operational performance."*

The OT&E section goes onto to describe the detail required at each milestone. Additionally, the OT&E section requires that test resources be based on scientifically defensible approaches with a reasonable level of test risk that is quantified in the TEMP.

Policy alone, however, is not enough to ensure full implementation of test science techniques, so DOT&E and DASD(DT&E) are working to ensure that the principles of Test Science are injected into in all guidance documents. The updated Defense Acquisition Guidebook (DAG) now provides a section on DOE that summarizes the key aspects of a DOE approach to testing; it highlights the importance of early engagement by all stakeholders, and summarizes the benefits of DOE as a test-planning tool.

In an October 2010 memorandum, DOT&E provided guidance on the level of detail they are looking for when reviewing TEMPs and test plans. The guidance highlights DOE as a scientific methodology that provides a defensible strategy for varying test conditions across multiple test events and within a single test event. DOT&E is looking for:

- The goal of the test,
- Quantitative, mission-oriented metrics,
- Factors and levels,
- Strategic methods for varying factors across the test continuum, and
- Statistical measures of merit (confidence and power) for metrics for which it makes sense.

DOT&E also published a TEMP Guidebook highlighting the substantive content we are looking for in TEMPs and Test Plans. This guidance is available on the DOT&E public website (www.dote.osd.mil). Specifically, it provides guidance on many test science topics including:

- Design of Experiments
- Mission-oriented metrics
- Reliability growth
- Modeling and Simulation
- Information Assurance

Test science topics have also been incorporated into other guidance documents including the T&E Management Guide and the Guide on Incorporating T&E into DoD Acquisition Contracts, which requires that test assets are *"determined by experimental design and analysis (such as DOE) or equivalent analysis, necessary to support the stated performance confidence levels."*

The Service OTAs are also implementing policy and guidance that support the use of DOE in operational testing. In 2009, all of the Service OTAs and DOT&E signed a memorandum of agreement (MOA) on DOE in operational testing. The MOA endorsed "DOE as a discipline to improve the planning, execution, analysis, and reporting of integrated testing." The MOA noted that "DOE offers a systematic, rigorous, data-based approach to test and evaluation."

AFOTEC's Initial Test Design process has included the use of experimental design techniques for many years now. During the past two years, other Service OTAs have updated and expanded their guidance and best practice documents to include DOE and other test science topics.

JITC has included a DOE Annex into the JITC Operational Test and Evaluation Guidebook. Additionally, they are adding a section on scientific test rigor to their Operations Research Systems Analysis guidebook that is currently under revision.

ATEC issued a policy bulletin in March 2012 that allows them to address DOT&E guidance on DOE. The bulletin establishes the DOE Support Analysis (DOESA) Cell. It outlines 10 key DOE products and a process, including all stakeholders, for implementing DOE in the test and evaluation process.

COTF established the DOE Working Group (DWG) Review Process in the Policy and Information Notice (PIN) 12-01 in February 2012. The new process formally integrates DOE into the existing Integrated Evaluation Framework (IEF) and requires an earlier review of the technical details of the design. Additionally, COTF has updated their IEF checklist to capture DOE best practices, including definitions for response variables, factor selection, and a methodology for prioritizing factors for consideration in the experimental design.

Recommendations

DOT&E, DASD(DT&E), and all of the Service OTAs have taken steps to incorporate scientific rigor into their test planning guidance over the past two years. They should continue to update these documents to incorporate best practices and lessons learned as the test and evaluation community learns more about the challenges and successes of incorporating statistical and scientific rigor into test and evaluation. DOT&E will continue to update the DOT&E TEMP Guidebook; in fact, we expect the next version of the TEMP Guidebook to be released shortly, incorporating lessons learned and new guidance since the original version was released in 2012.

This page intentionally left blank.

Section Four
Education and Training

Training and education are essential elements of the Test Science Roadmap. Over the past several years, all of the OTAs have included more statistical design and analysis techniques in the training they provide. The OTAs should continue to make training opportunities available to their workforce. DOT&E will continue to provide semi-annual training to DOT&E Action Officers, and always welcomes other members of the T&E community to attend these trainings. However, training itself is not enough to ensure that each test organization is adequately equipped to institutionalize scientific rigor in their test and evaluation processes. Each of the OTAs should seek more individuals with advanced degrees in applied statistics, operations research, and systems engineering.

Training and education, while related, are not the same. Training focuses on familiarization with concepts and knowledge of specific tools and processes for completing specific tasks or duties. Training tends to be of short duration, but quite often will cover a broad range of topics. Education, on the other hand, explores the underlying principles of the techniques and methods. The timeframe for educational courses is much longer, providing an acclimation period and time for reflection on the material and how it all fits together. This section will focus on training available to T&E professionals, but highlights one educational opportunity at the Air Force Institute of Technology (AFIT) because of its direct relationship to T&E.

All of the OTAs should employ individuals trained in DOE, statistical analysis methods, reliability planning and analysis, and other test science topics. Over the past two years, DOT&E has offered several training opportunities, including:

- Design and Analysis of Experiments
- Reliability Growth Planning
- Reliability Analysis
- Survey Design and Analysis

DOT&E Action Officers are trained semi-annually on these topics, and members of the broader test community are welcome in these training opportunities, especially the OTAs. A brief summary of available training resources from DOT&E is provided below. A subset of these training materials is provided in the Appendix of this report. Most of these training materials are available on the DOT&E Extranet site: https://extranet.dote.osd.mil.

DOT&E Action Officer Training

DOT&E New Action Officer Training – Design of Experiments (Appendix 1-1)

DOT&E provides annual training to new action officers on a variety of topics; starting in 2010, DOE was added as a targeted training topic. The course provides a general overview of DOE, focusing on the planning stages of DOE. It emphasizes the aspects of test planning that are important to document in TEMP and Test Plan development to ensure that the scientific context of the design is captured. It also helps action officers understand the wide variety of test designs that exist so that they can have an extensive toolkit available when reviewing TEMPs and Test Plans. The course also provides an overview of statistical analysis techniques for analyzing data from a designed experiment. The analysis section highlights various analysis techniques available and their relative applicability to the different types of tests. Although the course is not a comprehensive overview, it helps action officers appreciate the need for and benefits of advanced statistical analysis techniques.

DOT&E New Action Officer Training – Survey Design (Appendix 1-2)

The survey design briefing is part of the DOT&E annual new action officer training. The briefing provides an overview of how and when to use surveys in operational testing. It addresses when using surveys are appropriate. They are appropriate for measuring thoughts, workload, usability, and similar concepts, but they are not appropriate to measure physical requirements, accuracy, or situational awareness. The briefing discusses the "5 Golden Rules" for writing surveys, discusses appropriate and effective response types, and summarizes best practices for formatting surveys.

DOT&E New Action Officer Training – Reliability Growth (Appendix 1-3)

As a system is developed, there should be a plan to improve the reliabiltiy of the system over time. This requires testing to determine the system's "failure modes" and a funded plan to modify the system to eliminate failure modes. This briefing addressed concepts such as why there is a focus on reliability growth, reliabilty growth planning curves, and lessons learned from recent programs that made unrealistic assumptions regarding reliability growth.

DOT&E Warfare Brownbag Briefings (Appendix 1-4)

The four DOT&E Warfare (Air, Land, Naval, and Net-Centric and Space Systems) Brownbag briefings capture short, current examples of DOE in operational test plans and TEMPs. They often served as a starting point for internal discussion on test science topics. The presentations provide a brief overview of experimental design including the key elements action officers should evaluate in when reviewing TEMPs. Each overview is followed by a series of examples to facilitate discussion, spanning all warfare areas.

Additional Training Opportunities

Defense Acquisition University (DAU) Continuous Learning Module on Probability and Statistics

A baseline level of statistical literacy is essential to take advantage of all other trainings that assume a basic understanding of statistical concepts. However, until recently the DAU-provided continuous learning module (CLM) was outdated and failed to adequately prepare T&E professionals with baseline statistics knowledge. DOT&E, in collaboration with the DASD(DT&E), Virginia Polytechnic Institute and State University, and several T&E organizations, has updated the DAU probability and statistics CLM. The updated course became available in December 2012, providing a college-level introduction to statistics. This course is now required by the T&E Functional Integrated Product Team for Level I T&E certification and is prerequisite for the DAU course Test 203.

Eglin Design of Experiments Courses

The 53rd Wing and 96th Test Squadron at Eglin Air Force Base offer nine different training courses on DOE, ranging from a short executive overview to a week-long advanced topics course. Analysts across the test and evaluation community will benefit from taking the three one-week training courses: DOE I, DOE II, and DOE III. The courses are available to all DoD personnel (military and civilian) free of charge. These courses are also available to advisory and support contractors, with government client approval.

AFIT Science of Test Courses

AFIT offers three different training courses on the science of test (SOT). SOT 210 provides an introduction to DOE. SOT 310 provides an overview of the DOE foundational methods and techniques. SOT 410 is an intermediate experimental design course.

Acceptance Testing versus Rejection Testing (Appendix 2-1)

DOT&E asked IDA to develop a briefing on acceptance and rejection hypothesis testing. The briefing provides an overview for setting up hypothesis tests and makes recommendations for the appropriate methodology. It concludes that rejection-based hypotheses tests are more rigorous than acceptance-based tests, but not always applicable.

Power Calculations (Appendix 2-2)

Power calculations are essential for determining test adequacy in a statistical sense. They provide a quantitative tradeoff between test resources and risk. However, power calculations are generally not well understood, and they are implemented differently in different statistical packages, leading to more confusion. The IDA power calculations briefing summarizes methods and best practices, and highlights differences between software packages. Additionally, DOT&E supported IDA's development of a paper explaining power calculations, providing formulas and software code for practitioners.

What does DOE Buy Us? (Appendix 2-3)

This IDA tutorial explains why DOE should be used when conducting testing. It provides an introduction to regression analysis, a statistical analysis method that capitalizes on the benefits of the designed experiment. A straightforward test and evaluation example, in which data are collected using a designed experiment and analyzed using regression, illustrates the benefits of using DOE. The briefing compares a DOE-based analysis method to long-used methods for characterizing test results, such as a global mean, or case-by-case means. The comparison highlights the information gained using DOE.

Other Training Efforts

In addition to the training opportunities described above, DOT&E has collaborated with the OTAs to provide on-site training on a variety of topics ranging from DOE to advanced statistical methods that include censored data analysis, which is discussed in more detail in the Best Practices section of this report.

Educational Opportunities

As the OTA workforce study demonstrated, all of the OTAs could benefit by increasing their numbers of individuals educated in targeted fields (statistics, operations research, and industrial systems engineering). However, hiring these individuals in the current fiscal environment is not always possible. It is possible to grow these individuals from within the organization by making educational opportunities available to them. AFIT has created a certificate program that specifically targets the needs of DoD testers in a five-course, graduate-level program geared directly to DoD T&E personnel. Many universities also have excellent programs in applied statistics, operations research, and/or systems engineering that fill this educational need. Advanced degrees (Master's/Ph.D.s) are normally necessary to get to the conceptual statistical understanding needed for T&E.

AFIT Certificate Program

The AFIT Test and Evaluation Certificate Program (TECP) provides students with a fundamental understanding in the basic concepts required for supporting analysis in the test and evaluation community. TECP is a graduate-level program focused on the application of operational analysis techniques and methodology as applied to T&E. Particular emphasis is given to incorporating past, present, and future DoD T&E examples from all aspects of test (developmental, operational, etc.) into the curriculum to tailor the applications of the methodology and approaches within each course. The program provides an understanding of analysis tools dedicated to supporting the evaluation of test data, test design, and test execution. Additionally, current T&E focus areas, including DOE and reliability, maintainability, and availability (RM&A) analysis, are addressed in required courses. For further information on admission to the TECP, visit the Office of Admissions website at, http://www.afit.edu/en/admissions.

Recommendations

Education and training are essential for ensuring that scientific rigor results in improved test planning and analysis of system capabilities. All OTAs should continue to make training opportunities available to their workforces. DOT&E will continue to provide semi-annual training to action officers, and always welcomes other members of the T&E community to attend. However, training by itself is not enough to ensure that each test organization is adequately equipped to institutionalize scientific rigor in their test and evaluation processes. The OTAs should seek out individuals with advanced degrees in applied statistics, operations research, or systems engineering.

Currently there is no standard reference handbook or guidebook that captures best practices for incorporating statistics in T&E. DOT&E is working to develop a handbook that can be used by the entire T&E community. The handbook will capture statistically-based test approaches to answering common T&E questions and corresponding analysis methods.

Section Five
Case Studies

Case studies are essential in illustrating the application of complex scientific techniques to actual program tests. In fact, when DOT&E first advocated for the use of DOE in TEMPs and Test Plans, the first step was to investigate several case studies reviewing previous TEMPs and Beyond Low-Rate Initial Production (BLRIP) reports to illustrate exactly how DOE might apply to operational test and evaluation. During the past two years, the Test Science Roadmap Committee has held regular meetings where the OTAs and DOT&E have presented case studies illustrating the application of DOE to operational tests. Brownbag lunches have also been held with each of the DOT&E Warfare areas to discuss case studies and best practices. Finally, IDA has developed several case studies for DOT&E. These case studies have highlighted challenges, areas where more research is needed, and best practices. This section summarizes a representative sampling of these case studies, which span all of the Services and a variety of different types of systems. The full case studies are available in the appendices of this document, or by request. Additionally, the case studies are posted on the DOT&E Extranet site at: https://extranet.dote.osd.mil.

Test Science Roadmap Case Studies

Examples of DOE Applied in Air Warfare OT (Appendix 3-1)

These briefings contain two Air Force case studies, the Air Force Maverick Air-to-Ground Missile and the F-15 Operational Flight Program (OFP) upgrade. The primary objective of the Maverick test was to verify the success of a software correction. In previous testing, the system demonstrated a performance shortfall and was unable to lock onto targets under certain conditions. The analysis illustrates that the software correction significantly increased acquisition slant range under the conditions of interest. Additionally the test was able to characterize performance across a variety of conditions for both software versions.

The F-15 OFP case study illustrates how DOE can be used to accomplish multiple test objectives. In this example, 12 separate experimental designs are constructed separately to address each test objective. Each test plan is tuned independently to balance test risk with the overall importance of the objective. Using an experimental design approach saves approximately 10 percent over previously planned testing and results in a statistically defensible test program for all of the objectives.

DOE at MCOTEA – Global Combat Support System (Appendix 3-2)

The Global Combat Support System-Marine Corps (GCSS-MC) case study highlights the applicability and limitations of DOE and statistical methods for business systems. A primary objective in the GCSS-MC case study was to compare the performance of the new system to the legacy system. Observational study techniques, using selective data mining were used to objectively compare legacy system performance to a new system without resorting to a formal side-by-side test, which was infeasible. Additionally, the case study illustrates the use of nonparametric analysis methods to analyze data from the test because the data violate standard regression assumptions.

F-22 FOT&E 3.1 Test Design (Appendix 3-3)

The F-22 Case Study provides an overview of applying DOE to OT&E. The objective of the case study is to characterize system effectiveness. The case study capitalizes on sequential experimental design techniques to refine the test design based on previous testing. The case study presents an original design that is based on the AFOTEC test design process. A second design is developed as a reduced version of the first, and is based on eliminating a non-significant factor. This is an excellent example of how DOE can be used to support integrated testing and focus test resources.

ATEC Case Study (Appendix 3-4)

The ATEC Case Study provides an example of leveraging state-of-the-art statistical tools to design a statistically defensible test that meets operational testing needs and restrictions. The case study summarizes a test design for a cannon-delivered, GPS-guided projectile system. The objective of the test was to characterize the systems performance through the measurement of circular error probable (CEP) across the operational envelope. The test design leverages optimal design methodologies to account for test range restrictions and preserve operational realism. The case study also captures the benefits of early involvement between statisticians and all of the program stakeholders. In this case study, this early involvement contributed to a successful test planning process.

SPY-1D Radar Developmental Testing (Appendix 3-5)

The SPY-1D Radar case study provides a retrospective look at the developmental testing of the radar. The goal of the testing is to characterize detection, tracking, and engagement of low observable, low altitude targets in littoral environments. The executed test approach was a one-factor–at-a-time approach, which required 2,880 test points. Additionally, the executed test replicated every set of conditions 10-20 runs to achieve adequate power using individual hypothesis tests. Using DOE and a model-based analysis approach reduced the required runs by a factor of ten. This case study illustrates how doing bin-by-bin hypothesis tests is a costly approach to testing.

IDA Background Case Studies

DOE in TEMPs, T&E Concepts, Test Plans, and BLRIPS (Appendix 4-1)

This briefing compiled by IDA for DOT&E investigates seven past BLRIPs spanning a two-year period from 2008-2010, including the Stryker Mobile Gun System, *Virginia* Class Submarine, and Joint Chemical Agent Detector. It was intended to illustrate how the use of DOE, had it been used to develop the original test design, could have afforded testing efficiencies or provided an improvement in knowledge about system performance across the operational envelope. The briefing highlights that there are several elements that make a defensible test plan, including mission-oriented metrics, clear identification of the factors that define the operational envelope, a description of the coverage of the operational envelope, and statistical properties of the test design including confidence and power. The briefing provides several examples of how to illustrate the experimental design and document the design in TEMPs and Test Plans. These case studies were key in the development of the DOT&E guidance on the use of DOE in TEMPs and Test Plans.

Case Studies for the Use of DOE in Developmental Testing (Appendix 5-1)

This white paper on the use of DOE in DT provides a collection of case studies highlighting the applicability of DOE in DT. DT testing includes many different types of testing. In the white paper, IDA examines the use of DOE in a variety of test situations including trade studies, engineering analyses, assessment of material properties, accelerated life tests, software testing, interoperability, and characterizing performance. OT, tends to focus heavily on characterizing performance. The paper illustrates that DOE applies in all types of testing situations. The white paper concludes that not only is DOE applicable in DT, it additionally provides a wide range of benefits – systematic coverage of the test envelope, improved testing with faster detection of problems, potential cost and time efficiencies, and the ability to quantify the risks inherent to any test program.

Joint Chemical Agent Detector (JCAD) Test Design (Appendix 4-2)

The JCAD case study captures a series of four tests and summarizes best practices and lesions learned across all four tests. Chemical agent detectors are tested against real agents in a chamber. These chambers allow for the control of the factors that affect performance, making the application of DOE to the test program ideal. The JCAD case study provides an example of how using a related continuous variable, time to detect, enables significant testing efficiencies over the metric specified in the requirements document, probability to detect. During the first iteration of the test program, evaluators in the Army's OTA were not fully comfortable with using a statistical model (the DOE approach) to size the test; nor were they comfortable using the continuous metric. The result was unnecessary replication at each set of test conditions (16 for each, making the total test program more than 10,000 data points). IDA's analysis of the data employed the use of a statistical model and used a continuous metric: time to detect. The IDA analysis concluded that the test design was too large. Follow-on test designs and evaluations of the detector took advantage of the efficiencies afforded by switching to a continuous variable. The test design was reduced to 6 replicates per test point, resulting in a test program with less than 1,000 total data points.

Mobile Gun System (MGS) Case Study (Appendix 4-3)

The Mobile Gun System retrospective case study illustrates how DOE brings structure to operational testing using force-on-force exercises. The goal of the test was to determine if the new system provided increased operational capability to the users while ensuring operational realism. The retrospective study shows that test resource allocation could have been improved if DOE had been used in the planning process. Additionally, the case study illustrates how separate test designs should be used to address the separate missions of the MGS.

Apache Block III Case Study (Appendix 4-4)

The Apache Block III helicopter case study provides another example of conducting a designed experiment in an operational test. The case study covers all stages of the DOE process from planning to analysis. It highlights challenges in applying traditional experimental design methods to operational testing and how to overcome those challenges. The analysis of the experimental design provides an interesting result; expecting Apache helicopter pilots to control an unmanned aircraft system can actually hinder mission success. The case study concludes with lessons learned for future testing, including a discussion of how the very noisy data should be used to drive signal-to-noise ratios in future testing.

Integrated Defensive Electronic Countermeasures (IDECM) Case Study (Appendix 4-5)

The IDECM case study showcases a test design for an operational assessment whose goal is to characterize performance and screen for important factors prior to IOT&E. The case study highlights the importance of selecting appropriate response variables and factors. Advanced statistical design techniques (split-plot designs) are used to construct a design with restricted randomization based on operationally realistic sorties. Additionally, this case study illustrates best practices for making real-time decisions during a test when data loss or restrictions on testing become a reality.

Mine Susceptibility Testing (Appendix 5-2)

The mine susceptibility case study compares multiple design methodologies for the mine susceptibility test of the *Lewis and Clark* Class (T-AKE-1) Dry Cargo/Ammunition Ship using the Advanced Mine Simulation System (AMISS). The comparison study examines the trade space between the number of test conditions (factors) examined, the sample size (test cost), and the associated test risk. The case study compares seven different statistically valid designs to determine the trade-off between sample size and statistical power, which is a measure of test risk. The comparison study shows that designs between 20 and 28 test points are adequate to fully characterize the susceptibility of T-AKE-1 against AMISS as a function of range, ship speed, and whether or not the degaussing system is turned on.

Excalibur Logistic Regression (Appendix 4-7)

The Excalibur case study shows how advanced statistical analysis techniques can be used to characterize performance across a continuum of testing spanning several years. The case study identifies potential causes of system failure. However, true cause and effect cannot be determined without a designed experiment or the supporting engineering analysis.

Stryker Reliability Case Study (Appendix 4-8)

The Stryker case study illustrates the benefits of using parametric statistical models to combine information across multiple test events. Reliability is an essential element of system suitability. However, in the current era of constrained budgets and increasing reliability requirements, it is challenging to verify reliability requirements during an IOT&E. Both Bayesian and Non-Bayesian inference techniques are employed and contrasted to illustrate different statistical methods for combining information. These models leverage information from both developmental and operational test data for the Stryker Armored Vehicle. The case study illustrates how the conclusions of the reliability analysis would have differed if these parametric models had been used at the conclusion of the IOT&E.

Survey Case Study – Measuring Workload and Operator Latency: Command and Control Dynamic Targeting Cell (Appendix 4-9)

The survey case study shows the applicability of DOE and statistical analysis when the primary response is measured by a workload survey. The case study examines operator performance and workload for participants deploying assets to attack enemy targets and their ability to concurrently monitor auditory or visual communications in three conditions of time-pressure (low, medium, and high). The results show an increase in operator workload and a decrease in operator performance under high time-pressure conditions, especially when operators had to process multiple sources of information.

Joint Air-to-Ground Missile (JAGM) Test Concept

The JAGM case study provides an experimental design solution for characterizing the performance of a weapon system with a highly complex operational envelope. Optimal design methodologies are used to narrow the test design from 1,080 potential targeting conditions to a feasible test of 68 shots. The test design accounts for constraints on the operational envelope, including nested factors. The JAGM Test Concept is part of a larger IDA document and therefore not included in the Appendix; a copy is available upon request.

KC-46 Test Concept

The KC-46 case study provides a test concept for characterizing the aerial refueling capabilities of the new platform throughout its normal operational envelope relative to 18 receiver aircraft. An experimental design approach results in a feasible number of test events while yielding high power for detecting the effects of different conditions across the operational envelope, including various lighting conditions, operational tempo, receiver formations, and refueling altitudes and airspeeds. Using a D-optimal design methodology, a test with 48 tanker sorties and 84 fighter sorties yields high power for the main operational effects. The KC-46 Test Concept is part of a larger IDA document and therefore not included in the Appendix; a copy is available upon request.

Joint and Allied Threat Awareness System (JATAS) Test Concept

The JATAS case study provides an example of using experimental design in an integrated test paradigm. The experimental designs presented in the test design concept covers 12 test phases ranging from using the JATAS digital system model to flight testing. The majority of the test designs are based on D-optimality. In addition, a few small factorial designs are used for the live fire weapons tests. The overall design supports evaluation of main effects and two-way factor interactions with greater than 99 percent power for each model term at the 80 percent confidence level, with low correlations between model terms. These high powers are achieved primarily through careful design and a large number of replicates, but also by transforming the primary response variable (probability of a timely threat declaration) into a continuous variable (time to declare threats). The JATAS Test Concept is part of a larger IDA document and therefore not included in the Appendix; a copy is available upon request.

Kiowa Warrior Test Concept

The Kiowa Warrior test concept outlines a plan for applying DOE for developmental and operational testing. Factorial designs are used to span the operational envelope with adequate statistical power. Additionally the Kiowa Warrior test concept integrates effectiveness and suitability evaluations in a combined test plan strategy. The Kiowa Warrior Test Concept is part of a larger IDA document and therefore not included in the Appendix; a copy is available upon request.

Joint Space Operations Center (JSpOC) Mission System (JMS) Test Concept

The JSpOC JMS case study provides an example of applying experimental design to a software-intensive system to support the evaluation of operational effectiveness and suitability. Using DOE principles, the case study shows that the operational envelope can be covered during OT using a fractional factorial test design for the most important factors affecting the Critical Operational Issue (COIs). Eighteen unique factor-level combinations are considered for the effectiveness COIs and 16 unique factor-level combinations are considered for suitability COIs. A test design with high confidence and power for each of the KPPs can be validated with 17 test days for effectiveness and 8 days for suitability. The JSpOC JMS Test Concept is part of a larger IDA document and therefore not included in the Appendix; a copy is available upon request.

P-8A Test Design Study

Although the IOT&E planning for the P-8A had been complete and agreed to some years earlier, DOT&E asked IDA to use DOE techniques to determine a more efficient and thorough execution plan for the IOT&E using the already allocated resources in the TEMP. The P-8 test program was limited to the use of Fleet training exercises to provide the necessary data for the operational evaluation. The case study employed DOE under these constraints to ensure adequate test would be conducted under all the conditions of interest. The case study also provides an example of using DOE to develop a defensible test for comparing to the baseline legacy system. The use of DOE revealed the need for additional torpedo employment events, and enabled test efficiency by leveraging the resources from the torpedo test program. The result was a statistically adequate test design at no additional cost to the Navy. The P-8A Test Design is part of a larger IDA document and therefore not included in the Appendix; a copy is available upon request.

Fuel Leakage Comparative Analysis (Appendix 5-3)

The fuel leakage analysis case study investigates the impact of fuel type on the self-sealing properties of aircraft fuel bladders. The objective of the test was to collect data to determine if switching fuel types, from traditional petroleum-based fuels with high aromatic contents to bio-fuels negatively affects self-sealing. Four fuels were considered in the experiment, JP-5, JP-8, hydrotreated renewable jet fuel (HRJ-5), and a 50/50 blend of JP-5 and HRJ-5. The analysis used linear mixed modeling, an advanced statistical analysis technique, to determine if the fuel type affected the leakage rate for the data under consideration. The case study concludes that there was no statistical difference between three of the four fuel types: JP-8, HRJ-5, and the 50/50 blend. Additionally, the analysis showed that all of the fuel types exhibited some degree of self-sealing within approximately two minutes.

Censored Data Analysis Briefing (Appendix 4-6)

The requirements for many systems are defined as probability-based, or binomial, metrics. Such metrics have inherently low statistical power, making testing expensive since a large number of events or test assets are required to ensure a meaningful measurement of the system's performance. Switching to a related continuous measure suffers from the inability to capture missed detections (or missed hits) or similar failures in the system's performance. This briefing illustrates the ability to use a related continuous metric in lieu of the binomial one, but maintains the ability to measure missed detections and report on the original probability-based requirement. The briefing provides simple examples of one-sample analysis and a DOE-based analysis with multiple factors in a test design using the advanced technique of censored data analysis. The technique not only affords more accurate determinations of system performance, but also can reduce test sizes from 20 to 60 percent, especially for designed experiments.

This page intentionally left blank.

Section Six
Best Practices and Areas for Improvement

During the past two years, we have captured many best practices in the successful implementation of statistical and scientific rigor in testing. These best practices are not currently routinely incorporated into test design and analysis, but should be incorporated in all future tests.

Best Practices

Any program that applies scientific principles should commence doing so early in the test planning process. The program should assemble a test and evaluation working integrated product team (T&E WIPT) of all program stakeholders, including the program manager, the requirements representative, developmental and operational testers, and subject matter experts in experimental design and analysis. When formed early with clear objectives, the T&E WIPT can work to focus the test strategy and integrate the strategy across all phases of test to obtain maximum output for each dollar spent.

The T&E WIPT should identify the key elements of test planning identified by DOT&E's guidance on the use of experimental design in T&E. Additionally, the T&E WIPT should think strategically about how to incorporate new knowledge about system performance after each test. The testing strategy should be iterative in nature, accumulating evidence of system performance before and during IOT&E, to ensure an adequate IOT&E.

Several specific analytical best practices ensure efficient and effective testing while reducing the test resource footprint. These best practices include the following:

- Where possible, use continuous metrics as the primary measures of system performance as opposed to pass/fail probability-based metrics. Using continuous metrics has been shown to reduce test resource requirements by at least 30 to 50 percent for the same level of information.

- Use continuous factors when possible to cover the operational envelope with fewer test points. Identifying these continuous factors, or casting operational conditions in a continuous manner, enables the use of advanced test design techniques specifically available for continuous factors. Using these techniques will also afford test efficiencies and provide more information-rich test results.

- Use sequential experimentation approaches to reduce required test resources in each test phase, while developing a comprehensive view of system performance.

- When sizing tests, a single hypothesis test for determining statistical power is generally inadequate for ensuring that system performance is well-characterized in a test. When DOE is employed for test planning, the related factor-by-factor power calculations should be the primary focus for test sizing, vice a single "roll-up" power estimate.

- Test goals should not be limited to verifying a single narrowly-defined requirement in a static set of conditions. Rather, testing should aim to characterize performance of

31

the unit when equipped with the system across all feasible and operationally realistic conditions.

These best practices provide significant opportunities for cost savings while developing adequate and defensible test plans. However, it is not always trivial to employ these best practices. For example, consider a system designed to detect targets; we might suggest replacing the metric of probability of detection with an initial detection range, a continuous metric, so as to employ the best practice discussed above. However, the new metric does not account for missed detections, which is a primary focus of the testing. Rather than revert back to the probability-based metric (and the associated increase in test costs over a continuous metric), advanced statistical techniques can overcome these difficulties. Specifically for the missed-detection case, censored data analysis techniques would enable testers to use the continuous measure, but keep the missed detection information for characterizing system performance. Using that technique, we are able to capitalize on all data in the most efficient manner possible.

Another example of a challenge incurred by employing these best practices is answering the question of how to properly report on data obtained in developmental, integrated, and operational testing. Again, DOT&E is beginning to use advanced analysis techniques, including generalized linear models and Bayesian data analysis, when appropriate, to properly combine information across test phases.

Areas for Improvement

Despite the significant progress that has been made in the past two years, there is still work to be done before the T&E community is fully capitalizing on the complete toolset that the scientific community has available for T&E. The Service OTAs have modified their test design and planning techniques to incorporate DOE methodologies and take advantage of the efficiencies afforded by these methods. These changes have resulted in an improvement in the quality of the TEMPs and Test Plans that are based on these methods. However, two areas need to improve in the future as the Department institutionalizes statistical rigor in testing:

- Execution of testing in accordance with the planned test design.
- Analysis of test data using more advanced statistical methods that are commensurate with the DOE-based test designs.

For the former, DOT&E has seen some cases where a test is well-designed, but the desired conditions of the test in the field are not the same as required by the original plan. This has the effect of reducing the efficiency or limiting the conclusions that can be made from the subsequent data. Since most of our tests are focused on characterizing the performance of a system across the various conditions in which the operators will employ it, it is crucial that the planned conditions are achieved during the test.

Second, DOT&E has not yet observed all of the OTAs employing the data analysis methods that would reap the benefits of the efficiencies afforded by DOE methodologies. In other words, although the OTAs use statistical rigor in their test planning, they are not always following up with the same rigor in the analysis of test data. The simplest case of this is where a test is designed to cover all or many of the important operational conditions, and is optimized to be extremely efficient in the number of test iterations in each condition, but the data analysis is limited to reporting a single average (mean) of the performance across all the test conditions. This result throws away all of the careful test design efficiencies afforded by the DOE methodology. A more statistically rigorous analysis would enable analysts to extract much more information from the data, in order to state how well the system performed in each of the conditions it was tested under. The more advanced statistical analysis also enables statements of system performance to be made with higher confidence in many cases, so that acquisition decisions can be based on solid analytical evidence.

Recommendations

- Employ the best practices listed above.

- Test Execution should be in accordance with the planned test design to ensure that the efficiencies afforded by DOE methods are not lost and the ability to characterize system performance is maintained.

- The test data should be analyzed using the statistical methods that are commensurate with the test design.

This page intentionally left blank.

Section Seven
The Role of T&E in Requirements

The best practices and lessons learned over the past two years have the potential not only to improve testing but also, if incorporated by the requirements community, to improve the analytical link between test and requirements. This section provides a summary of DOT&E's efforts to engage the requirements community over the past year as a result of lessons learned in employing scientific methods in test design and analysis.

Three specific areas where increased interactions between the test and requirements communities could result in improved test outcomes are discussed below.

Mission-Oriented Metrics

Operational test and evaluation is defined in Title 10 United States Code, Section 139 as:

"the field test, under realistic combat conditions, of any item of (or key component of) weapons, equipment, or munitions for use in combat by typical military users; and the evaluation of the results of such tests."

Weapon systems sit in the motor pool, at the pier, or on the runway. Individual systems do not have missions; it takes soldiers, sailors, airmen, and Marines to make them work. Operational testing is about assessing mission accomplishment by units equipped with the system under test. To evaluate operational effectiveness, we seek to answer the question: "Can a unit equipped with the system under test show an improvement in unit mission accomplishment?" Operational effectiveness is defined in the Joint Capabilities Integration and Development System (JCIDS) manual as:

"Measure of the overall ability of a system to accomplish a mission when used by representative personnel in the environment planned or expected for operational employment of the system considering organization, doctrine, tactics, supportability, survivability, vulnerability and threat."

And the Defense Acquisition Guide emphasizes that "the evaluation of operational effectiveness is linked to mission accomplishment." End-to-end testing with operational users across the intended operational envelope is essential to assessing a system's impact on mission accomplishment. Additionally, the system must be evaluated in the context of the system-of-systems within which it will operate.

In January 2010, DOT&E provided guidance to the OTAs on the reporting of OT&E results, reiterating that the appropriate environment for operational evaluation includes not only the system under test, but all interrelated systems needed to accomplish an end-to-end mission in combat. The primary purpose of OT&E is to describe the operational effectiveness and suitability of the system under test. A second purpose of OT&E is to determine whether thresholds in the approved capabilities production documents have been satisfied. The Milestone Decision Authority needs this information in making production decisions. The measures used

35

for this purpose are appropriately referred to in the context of "performance," as in "key performance parameters" or "measures of performance." But these measures are not the military effectiveness or operational effectiveness measures required for achieving combat capability.

It is inadequate to evaluate and report on operational effectiveness and suitability by parsing requirements and narrowing the definition of mission accomplishment. Basing evaluation solely on performance parameters can obscure the fundamental fact that the system being fielded is not operationally effective or suitable when used in conjunction with interrelated systems in combat by a typical military crew or unit. A narrow focus can also lead to erroneously evaluating as operationally ineffective a system that fails to meet certain performance parameters but nonetheless provides measurable improvement in mission accomplishment.

Unfortunately, the goals of the operational evaluation often are not captured by the systems' requirements documents. Requirements are typically technical in nature. And while technical performance requirements are necessary, they are not sufficient for the evaluation of operational effectiveness, suitability, and survivability. Ideally, KPPs should provide a measure of mission accomplishment, lend themselves to good test design, and encapsulate the reasons for procuring the system. DOT&E has seen many recent examples of KPPs that are not informative towards the evaluation of mission accomplishment. For example, a ground combat vehicle had KPPs that only required it to seat nine passengers, be transportable by a C-130, and have specific radio system; these requirements could have been met by a passenger van. Another example was an amphibious ship with KPPs for the number of helicopter spots, the number of storage spaces, and the maximum speed of the ship; these requirements could have been measured with a stopwatch and a tape measure. While these technical performance requirements are important, they are often not really key or relevant; they do not capture the actual mission of the ground vehicle or ship. For these examples, the test community encouraged the use of mission-oriented metrics such as improving combat outcomes in force-on-force missions or meeting an aircraft sortie generation rate and adding self-defense capabilities. If the test community and the requirements community engage early, these measures can be fleshed out to ensure that testable requirements are used more directly in the determination of operational effectiveness.

Leveraging T&E knowledge in setting requirements

Interactions between requirements writers and testers can help identify alternatives to hard-to-test requirements. Very high requirements are difficult and costly to test with confidence. If high performance is truly needed, the program must consider the engineering and test cost implications for designing a system to such high tolerances.

The T&E community has knowledge of legacy system performance and capabilities that can provide useful inputs into the requirements-setting process. Testers can help identify unrealistic, unaffordable, and untestable requirements. Additionally, knowledge of the current threat environment and test infrastructure can help the requirements community understand what resources will be needed to test a given requirement. Service requirements officers often demand high requirements to drive vendors to produce the best possible system performance, but history has shown that unachievably high requirements can be destructive to program success in the long term. For example, a ground combat vehicle program needed both high survivability ("tank-like") and tactical transportability requirements (via C-130) that were not compatible because of the weight associated with the high survivability requirement. Additionally, reliability requirements for that same system were much higher (nearly 10 times) than that of our current systems, making it both unrealistic and unaffordable. Clearly, we should not eliminate requirements simply because they are difficult to test (consider, for example, body armor and combat helmets), but decision-makers who ratify such requirements should first be alerted to the need to understand the implications.

Testers have experience with the difficulty and cost associated with testing to certain metrics. For example, consider a requirement for 99-percent reliability for completing a 6-hour mission. This is comparable to 600 hours between failures and would require, at a minimum, 1,800 hours of testing. If the requirement were lowered to 95-percent reliability, the associated mean time between failures is only 120 hours and testing could be accomplished in a minimum of 350 hours. If the testing revealed 40 hours between failures (instead of 120 or 600), that would indicate an 86 percent probability of completing a 6-hour mission. Is this good enough? For evaluators to make this judgment, the rationale for the reliability requirement needs to be provided by the requirements writer. DOT&E intends to mandate that Milestone B TEMPs have an annex explaining the users' rationale for requirements in the Capability Development Document or the equivalent document. The requirements and rationale should be revisited as often as needed to permit discovery during the lifetime of the program.

Similar test cost considerations apply for performance testing; the T&E community notes that probability metrics are expensive to test because they require large sample sizes to gain statistical confidence in the results. However, if meaningful continuous metrics that relate to probability requirements can be derived, testers can significantly constrain test resources. For example, the "median miss distance" can be measured at high confidence with about a third the sample size of the "probability of hit," and also provides more information from the resulting distribution of measurements (how close or far away) than a simple hit/miss answer. Thus, wherever possible, DOT&E is mandating test plans that measure continuous performance variables as the medium for evaluation of thresholds that have been written in terms of probabilities.

Evaluation across the Operational Envelope

Another disconnect between the requirements community and the test community is that often requirements are narrowly focused and do not cover the operational envelope; a notional depiction is shown in Figure 7-1 below. The operational evaluation should report performance of the system across the operational envelope, not just at single conditions specified in the capabilities documents. One common concern is that failing to specify a certain set of conditions could lead to an unwieldy test. This is one of the reasons DOT&E is using DOE to efficiently span the operational envelope. Requirements can help inform the operational environment for testing by identifying multiple conditions where the system is likely to be operated.

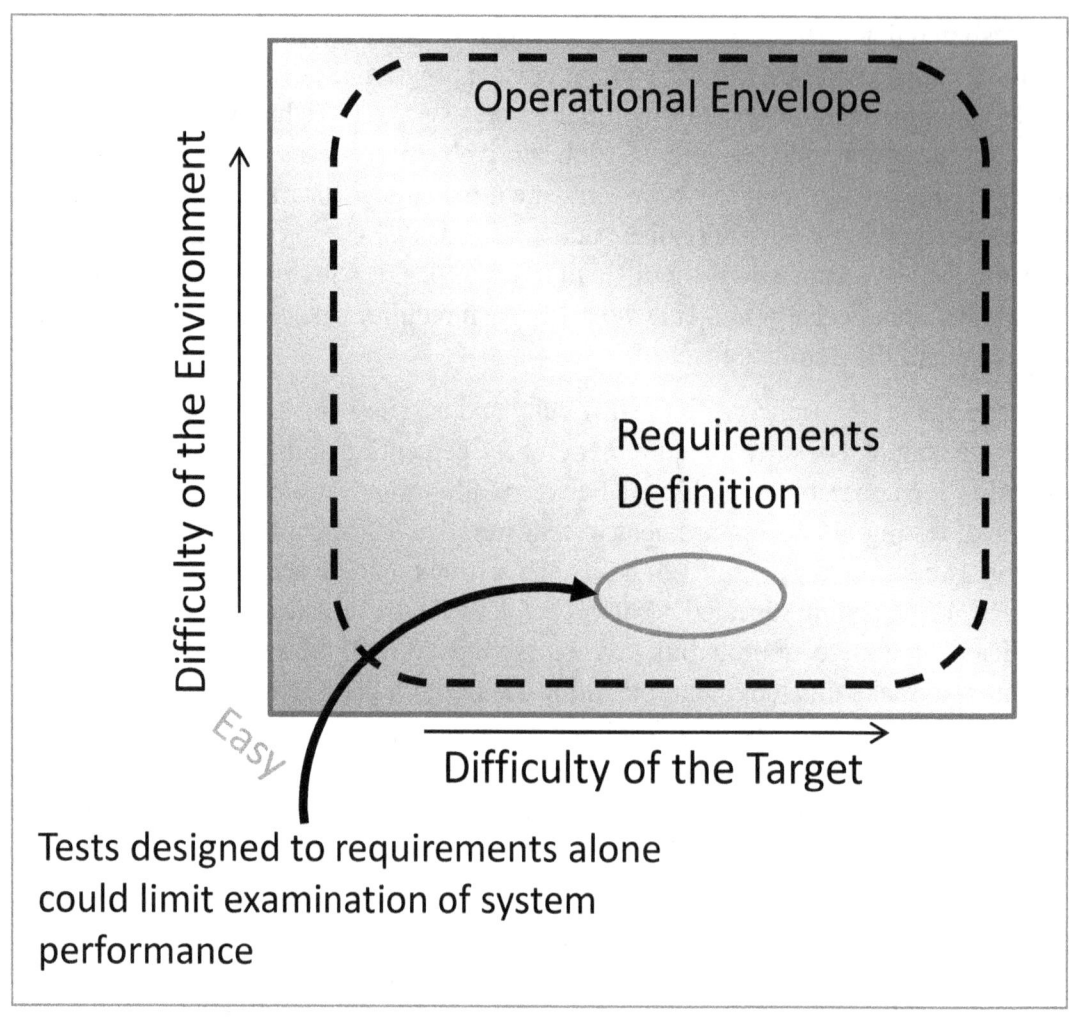

Figure 7-1. Notional two-dimensional diagram of a weapon system's operational envelope

DOT&E has advocated for the use of DOE as a scientific methodology for approaching the development of tests that span the operational envelope. One of the key tenets of a well-designed experiment is that all stakeholders must be engaged in the determination of the goals, metrics, operational envelope, and test risks. The requirements community is a key stakeholder in determining these test elements. The requirements community can provide valuable input on what the factors (or conditions) are that they expect will influence mission performance (and thus should be considered in operational test), and testers must select the best allocation of test resources to evaluate requirements across the operational envelope.

In summary, through early and continuous engagement between the testing and requirements communities, we can craft requirements that are mission-oriented, realistic, testable, and responsive to the limitations and opportunities that are revealed during system development. Additionally, the requirements community can provide valuable input on the test conditions that define the operational envelope.

Recommendations

DOT&E will continue to work to engage the requirements community in a discussion of how we can improve interactions between tests and requirements. In addition to providing briefings to members of the requirements community, DOT&E is participating in the development of DAU courses for the requirements community.

This page intentionally left blank.

Section Eight
Advisory Committee

The Roadmap Committee, consisting of technical representatives from DOT&E, DASD(DT&E), the OTAs, the Service T&E organizations, Federally Funded Research Development Centers, and academia, has served as an effective advisory board for the past two years. Regular meetings of this advisory committee should continue into the future to facilitate the exchange of knowledge across organizations. The advisory group should continue to share leadership perspective, best practices, case studies, lessons learned, and educational and training resources.

Additionally, two different application groups have been formed in the past two years. The first is the Science of Test Research Consortium. This consortium is academically based and provides high-level advice to the DoD on test science issues. The second is the Scientific Test and Analysis Techniques Test and Evaluation Center of Excellence (STAT T&E COE), charged with assisting active programs in the DoD. In essence, they are working to operationalize test science in active programs. Both groups are making great strides forward in improving test science in T&E. In the future, an annual meeting of the OSD advisory committee, the Science of Test Research Consortium, and the STAT T&E COE should be held to facilitate the exchange of ideas between organizational leadership, academic expertise, and practitioners. This section provides more background on the Science of Test Research Consortium and the STAT T&E COE.

Science of Test Research Consortium

The Science of Test Research Consortium is a consortium of four Universities: Air Force Institute of Technology (AFIT), Naval Postgraduate School (NPS), Arizona State University (ASU), and Virginia Polytechnic Institute and State University (VT). The consortium is sponsored by DOT&E and the DoD Test Resource Management Center (TRMC). The primary goal of the research consortium is to support the integration of advanced statistical and mathematical methods into DoD T&E in order to improve the "science of test" across the DoD. The unique academic expertise of the Research Consortium allows them to leverage cutting edge academic research to provide solutions to challenging problems facing the T&E community. Specifically, they are charged with:

- Conducting basic research on DOE,
- Making fundamental contributions to the statistically-valid test body of knowledge,
- Providing methods and processes for improving the statistical rigor of DoD T&E,
- Implementing advanced methodologies into practice using interested parties, and
- Supporting OSD and individual Service education and training.

Since 2011, the research consortium has made valuable contributions to the T&E community, including:

41

- Supporting workforce development--

  - Developing a new continuous learning module on probability and statistics for the Defense Acquisition University;

  - Developing training on DOE for IT systems.

- Performing doctoral-level research on:

  - Cost-optimal experimental design selection,

  - Bayesian experimental design,

  - Design and analysis of reliability experiments,

  - Supersaturated experimental designs,

  - Non-linear screening designs, and

  - Design and analysis for scarce data situations.

- Leveraging cutting-edge methodologies for T&E challenges--

  - Using response surface methodology to improve the design efficiency of the Aerial Refueling Airplane Simulator Qualification (ARASQ) flight test protocol for the KC-46 program.

  - Supporting vulnerability research by developing empirical modeling techniques for flash events that occur when missile fragments impact the fuselage of an aircraft.

Overall, the research consortium will have produced (or is in the process of producing) 16 peer-reviewed journal articles in the past year that will provide new methodologies and guidance to the T&E community. Additionally, the consortium has developed a website that, in the future, will provide a common infrastructure for disseminating cutting-edge research, best practices, and case studies to the T&E community.

Scientific Test and Analysis Techniques Center of Excellence

As previously noted, DASD(DT&E), in collaboration with DOT&E and the Service T&E Executives, signed an implementation plan in January of 2012, endorsing the use of scientific test and analysis techniques in T&E. A key aspect of this implementation plan was the establishment of a Center of Excellence (COE). The STAT T&E COE consists of five technical experts with acquisition and T&E experience. The STAT T&E COE provides a high level of scientific and statistical expertise not widely available within program offices. The STAT T&E COE has been directly involved in test planning for programs, influencing resources in the TEMP in a defensible manner. They are also providing training to the T&E community.

The STAT T&E COE is envisioned to provide long-term T&E capability for the acquisition community. Initially, the STAT T&E COE will support 20 programs providing scientific test planning, execution, and analysis assistance. The programs currently supported by the STAT T&E COE are:

- Air Force
  - Air Force Integrated Personnel and Pay System
  - B-61 Mod 12 Life Extension Program
  - Combat Rescue Helicopter
  - KC-46 Tanker Modernization
  - Space Fence
  - Air and Space Operations Center – Weapon System initiative 10.2
  - Space-Based Infrared System Program, High Component
- Army
  - Indirect Fire Protection Capability Increment 2 – Intercept
  - Common Infrared Countermeasures
  - Integrated Air and Missile Defense
  - Logistics Modernization Program
  - Armored Multipurpose Vehicle
  - Next Generation Diagnostics System
  - Stryker Engineering Change Proposal
- Navy
  - DDG-51 Flight III Guided Missile Destroyer
  - LHA-R Amphibious Assault Ship
  - Ship-to-Shore Connector
  - Distributed Common Ground System – Navy Increment 2
  - Next Generation Enterprise Network
  - Joint Precision Approach and Landing System

Future Directions

The establishment of the Science of Test Research Consortium and the STAT T&E COE are essential components of the Roadmap. The Research Consortium pushes the state-of-the-art of test science and provides novel solutions to the complex challenges that the T&E community faces. The STAT T&E COE works to implement test science at a programmatic level. However, more work remains. Increased collaboration between these two groups will be key for future success. The STAT T&E COE can provide concrete examples and problems to the Research Consortium, and in turn, the Research Consortium can provide new, unique solutions to the T&E community.

The Research Consortium has also developed a website that, once populated with information, will provide an excellent resource for the T&E community. However, they need content from the T&E community to make this website a success.

Finally, a formal linkage of these groups with the OSD-level advisory group in the future will ensure a continuing exchange of idea. An annual meeting devoted to test science could provide a forum for these groups to get together and exchange ideas.

Section Nine
Recommendations and Future Directions

The Test Science Roadmap was a two-year effort that began in January 2011 to increase the statistical and scientific rigor in test and evaluation. There has been significant progress made in the past two years. Major accomplishments include: the establishment of the complementary DT&E, STAT Implementation Plan and the STAT T&E COE; the incorporation of scientific principles into T&E guidance at the OSD level and within the Service OTAs; the development of training to support T&E practitioners; the development of numerous case studies illustrating the benefits of DOE; and the establishment of advisory boards from which the T&E community can draw. However, there is still much work to be done before test science is institutionalized within the T&E community. The recommendations below suggest a future path for DOT&E, DT&E, and the individual Service test organizations.

Workforce Recruiting and Development

- All OTAs should work toward achieving a higher percentage of Science Technology Engineering and Mathematics (STEM) education backgrounds.

- OTAs should consider hiring (or developing from within) at least one, and ideally many, Ph.D.-level STEM civilians to their workforce.

  - Each OTA should have at least one subject matter expert on test design and analysis techniques.

Policy and Guidance

- DOT&E and DASD(DT&E) should continue to require a scientific approach to test planning in TEMPs and Test Plans (outlined in 5000.02 updates).

- DOT&E should continue regular updates of the TEMP Guidebook to reflect current best practices and lessons learned.

Education and Training

- Currently, no military handbook or written document exists to summarize best practices and statistical methods for T&E. A handbook on statistical methods for T&E should be developed.

- All test organizations should continue (or begin) hosting periodic training on DOE, statistical analysis, and reliability. DOT&E should continue to provide regular training, and will add more training on data analysis methods for test reporting.

- DOT&E should host (as soon as financially tenable) an annual conference/meeting on statistical methods for T&E. This conference will provide a forum for presenting case studies, best practices, and lessons learned, and for providing training opportunities.

Case Studies

- Continue to encourage the development and documentation of case studies and best practices.

- Make case studies and best practices publically available on an easy–to-navigate website.

Best Practices

- Use continuous metrics (whenever possible) as the primary measures of system performance as opposed to pass/fail probability-based metrics.

- Use continuous factors when possible to cover the operational envelope with fewer test points.

- Use sequential experimentation approaches to reduce required test resources in each test phase, while developing a comprehensive view of system performance.

- When sizing tests, use DOE-related factor-by-factor power calculations, vice a single "roll-up" power estimate.

- Plan tests to characterize performance across all feasible and operationally realistic conditions.

- Execute testing in accordance with the planned test design.

- Analyze test data using advanced statistical methods that are commensurate with the DOE-based test designs.

- Continue to research and apply state-of-the-art analysis methodologies that accommodate the complex challenges of T&E.

Advisory Committee

- DOT&E should continue to host a regular meeting of an OSD-level advisory board including technical representatives from DOT&E, DASD(DT&E), the OTAs, the Service T&E organizations, Federally Funded Research Development Centers, and academia.

- Develop a formal linkage of the OSD advisory group with the Science of Test Research Consortium and the STAT T&E COE. An annual meeting devoted to test science could provide a forum for these groups to get together and exchange ideas.